YOUR FREE SURPRISE GIFT!

HILARIOUS JOKES FOR CLEVER KIDS!
RATHER FUNNY PRESS

Details on the last page of this book!
A brand new free joke book
just for you.
Check it out! Laughter awaits!

KU-205-517

HOW TO PLAY

This easy to play game is a ton of fun!
Have 2 or more players.
The first reader will choose a 'Would You Rather?'
from the book and read it aloud.
The other player(s) then choose which scenario
they would prefer and why.
You can't say 'neither' or 'none'.
You must choose one and explain why.
Then the book is passed to the next person
and the game continues!

The main rule is have fun, laugh and enjoy
spending time with your friends and family.
Let the fun begin!

ATTENTION!

All the scenarios and choices in this book are
fictional and meant to be about using your
imagination, having a ton of fun and enjoying this
game with your friends and family.
Obviously, DO NOT ATTEMPT any of these
scenarios in real life.

RatherFunnyPress.com

WOULD YOU RATHER? FOR

10 YEAR OLD KIDS!

Includes a BONUS
EWW! YUCK! GROSS!
chapter at the end of this book!
HILARIOUS AND FUN!
RatherFunnyPress.com

Books By
RATHER FUNNY PRESS

Would You Rather? For 6 Year Old Kids!
Would You Rather? For 7 Year Old Kids!
Would You Rather? For 8 Year Old Kids!
Would You Rather? For 9 Year Old Kids!
Would You Rather? For 10 Year Old Kids!
Would You Rather? For 11 Year Old Kids!
Would You Rather? For 12 Year Old Kids!
Would You Rather? For Teens!
Would You Rather? Eww! Yuck! Gross!

To see all the latest books by Rather Funny Press just go to
RatherFunnyPress.com

WOULD YOU RATHER...

BE ABLE TO SPEAK TO DOGS

OR

SPEAK TO BABIES?

BE ABLE TO SEE YOUR OWN FUTURE

OR

BE ABLE TO SEE OTHER PEOPLE'S FUTURE BUT NOT YOURS?

WOULD YOU RATHER...

ADOPT A BABY MONKEY

OR

A BABY PENGUIN?

CONTROL YOUR DREAMS AS YOU ARE DREAMING

OR

BE ABLE TO WATCH YOUR DREAMS ON TV THE NEXT DAY?

WOULD YOU RATHER...

HAVE FINGERS ON
YOUR FEET

OR

TOES ON YOUR HANDS?

SWIM WITH A GOLDFISH THE
SIZE OF A WHALE

OR

100 WHALES THE SIZE OF
A GOLDFISH?

WOULD YOU RATHER...

WEAR WET SOCKS

OR

WET UNDERWEAR?

TIME TRAVEL 200 YEARS INTO THE PAST

OR

200 YEARS INTO THE FUTURE?

WOULD YOU RATHER...

DRINK SOUR MILK

OR

EAT A ROTTEN APPLE?

HAVE FINGERS AS LONG AS YOUR LEGS

OR

LEGS AS LONG AS YOUR FINGERS?

WOULD YOU RATHER...

WEAR A UNIFORM TO SCHOOL

OR

CASUAL CLOTHES?

SHARE YOUR ROOM WITH SOMEONE ELSE

OR

MOVE INTO THE ATTIC OR BASEMENT BY YOURSELF?

WOULD YOU RATHER...

CRY WHEN YOU SHOULD LAUGH

OR

LAUGH WHEN YOU SHOULD CRY?

LIVE IN A HOUSE FULL OF DOGS

OR

A HOUSE FULL OF CATS?

WOULD YOU RATHER...

SPEND EVERY WINTER AT THE SNOW

OR

EVERY SUMMER AT THE BEACH?

BE A KID FOR THE REST OF YOUR LIFE

OR

BE A GROWN UP NOW?

WOULD YOU RATHER...

HAVE THE EYES OF
A BAT

OR

THE WINGS OF A BAT?

CHANGE YOUR FIRST
NAME

OR

YOUR MIDDLE NAME?

WOULD YOU RATHER...

HAVE ONE HAND TWICE AS BIG AS USUAL

OR

HALF THE USUAL SIZE?

BE ABLE TO FLY

OR

BE ABLE TO TURN YOU AND YOUR FRIENDS INTO CARTOON CHARACTERS?

WOULD YOU RATHER...

BE AN
OLYMPIC ATHLETE

OR

THE PRESIDENT?

HAVE A 3D PRINTER YOU CAN
USE ALL THE TIME

OR

THE BEST CELL PHONE YOU
CAN GET?

WOULD YOU RATHER...

BE THE FASTEST SWIMMER IN THE WORLD

OR

THE FASTEST RUNNER IN THE WORLD?

BE FLUENT IN 5 LANGUAGES

OR

BE ABLE TO CODE IN 5 DIFFERENT PROGRAMMING LANGUAGES?

WOULD YOU RATHER...

EAT A DEAD COCKROACH

OR

GET STUNG BY A BEE?

ALWAYS WIN AT
MONOPOLY

OR

BE UNBEATABLE AT ROCK,
PAPER, SCISSORS?

WOULD YOU RATHER...

KISS A JELLYFISH

OR

LICK A ROTTEN FISH?

HAVE WATER BALLOONS THROWN AT YOU FOR 5 MINUTES

OR

TENNIS BALLS THROWN AT YOU FOR 2 MINUTES?

WOULD YOU RATHER...

SLIP ON A
BANANA PEEL

OR

TRIP OVER WHILE TRYING TO
AVOID THE BANANA PEEL?

EAT A BOWL OF SPAGHETTI
THAT WAS JUST ONE REALLY
LONG NOODLE

OR

EAT A BALL OF ICE CREAM
THAT SOMEONE THREW
INTO YOUR MOUTH?

WOULD YOU RATHER...

BE A WIZARD

OR

A SUPERHERO?

SPEAK EVERY LANGUAGE ON EARTH

OR

BE ABLE TO CHANGE THE COLOR OF ANYTHING WITH YOUR MIND?

WOULD YOU RATHER...

HAVE A FOOT LONG TONGUE

OR

A FOOT LONG NOSE?

SEE AN AMAZING FIREWORKS DISPLAY

OR

SPEND THE NIGHT AT THE CIRCUS?

WOULD YOU RATHER...

SEE A BEE THE SIZE OF
AN ELEPHANT

OR

AN ELEPHANT THE SIZE
OF A BEE?

NOT SHOWER FOR
A WEEK

OR

NOT CHANGE YOUR CLOTHES
FOR A WEEK?

WOULD YOU RATHER...

GO TO A WATER PARK

OR

AN AMUSEMENT PARK?

BE TRAPPED FOR 2 HOURS IN A ROOM FULL OF BEES

OR

SCORPIONS?

WOULD YOU RATHER...

NEVER PLAY VIDEO GAMES AGAIN

OR

NEVER EAT FAST FOOD AGAIN?

WALK THROUGH A HALLWAY FULL OF SNAKES

OR

A CAVE FULL OF SPIDERS?

WOULD YOU RATHER...

BE ABLE TO GLOW IN THE DARK

OR

SEE IN THE DARK?

HAVE A GENIE'S LAMP

OR

A TALKING DOG?

WOULD YOU RATHER...

BE A MOVIE STAR

OR

A YOUTUBE STAR?

HAVE A SPIDER CLIMB INTO YOUR BED

OR

A MOUSE CLIMB INTO YOUR BED?

WOULD YOU RATHER...

BUY VIDEO GAMES
ONLINE

OR

IN THE STORE?

HAVE A THREE-STORY
TREE HOUSE

OR

A THREE-STORY WATER SLIDE
INTO YOUR POOL?

WOULD YOU RATHER...

LISTEN TO THE SAME SONG ON REPEAT OVER AND OVER FOR A MONTH

OR

NOT LISTEN TO ANY MUSIC FOR A YEAR?

SWIM WITH DOLPHINS

OR

RIDE A CAMEL?

WOULD YOU RATHER...

HAVE A TIME MACHINE

OR

BE ABLE TO TALK TO
YOUR PET?

EAT SOME WEEDS TOPPED WITH
MELTED CHOCOLATE

OR

EAT A CHOCOLATE BAR
COATED IN MUD?

WOULD YOU RATHER...

BE ABLE TO CLICK YOUR FINGERS AND YOUR FAVORITE FOOD APPEARS

OR

YOUR BEST FRIEND APPEARS?

HAVE A PET DRAGON

OR

A PET UNICORN?

WOULD YOU RATHER...

HOLD A GIANT SPIDER

OR

A GIANT COCKROACH?

HAVE THE WORLD'S LARGEST CAR COLLECTION

OR

THE WORLD'S LARGEST VIDEO GAME COLLECTION?

WOULD YOU RATHER...

HAVE A BATH IN KETCHUP

OR

MELTED CHOCOLATE?

BE ABLE TO ONLY HEAR VERY QUIET SOUNDS

OR

VERY LOUD SOUNDS?

WOULD YOU RATHER...

HAVE TO READ FOR 6 HOURS A DAY

OR

NOT KNOW HOW TO READ AT ALL?

TAKE A SELFIE WITH A LLAMA

OR

A KANGAROO?

WOULD YOU RATHER...

HAVE TWO TONGUES

OR

NO TONGUE AT ALL?

HAVE A PET TALKING
DINOSAUR

OR

AN ALIEN AS YOUR BEST
FRIEND?

WOULD YOU RATHER...

BATTLE A RAT THE SIZE
OF A HIPPO

OR

20 HIPPOS THE SIZE OF
A RAT?

BE STUCK IN AN ELEVATOR
WITH 2 WET DOGS

OR

AN ELDERLY GENTLEMAN WITH
BAD BREATH?

WOULD YOU RATHER...

SLEEP NEXT TO A
SKUNK

OR

A BABY GIRAFFE?

EAT ONLY DONUTS FOR THE
NEXT WEEK

OR

HAVE ONE DONUT A MONTH FOR
THE REST OF YOUR LIFE?

WOULD YOU RATHER...

HAVE BRIGHT BLUE SKIN

OR

BRIGHT PINK SKIN?

HAVE MULTICOLORED STRIPED HAIR

OR

HAIR THAT SMELLS LIKE APPLE PIE?

WOULD YOU RATHER...

BE A DOCTOR

OR

TEACHER?

LIVE IN THE SKY IN A FLOATING APARTMENT

OR

LIVE UNDERWATER IN A PARKED SUBMARINE?

WOULD YOU RATHER...

HAVE AN ACTION FIGURE THAT WALKS

OR

A TOY THAT TALKS?

HAVE A CUDDLE WITH A SMALL BEAR

OR

A LARGE COYOTE?

WOULD YOU RATHER...

HAVE YOUR GRANDMA
THROW UP ON YOU

OR

YOU THROW UP ON YOUR
GRANDMA?

DRINK MILK LIKE A CAT BY
LICKING A BOWL OF MILK

OR

CLEAN YOURSELF BY LICKING
LIKE A CAT?

WOULD YOU RATHER...

MEET A DOG THAT WALKS
UPRIGHT ON TWO LEGS

OR

A DOG THAT TALKS?

DANCE AROUND YOUR HOUSE
IN YOUR UNDERWEAR

OR

DANCE AROUND THE
NEIGHBOURHOOD WEARING YOUR
UNDERWEAR AS A HAT?

WOULD YOU RATHER...

HAVE A RABBIT'S EARS

OR

A RAT'S TEETH?

MAKE REALLY LOUD BURPS THAT DON'T SMELL

OR

VERY QUIET BURPS THAT SMELL REALLY BAD?

WOULD YOU RATHER...

WEAR A CLOWN NOSE

OR

CLOWN SHOES FOR THE
REST OF YOUR LIFE?

HAVE A UNICORN OF YOUR OWN
THAT YOU CAN TALK TO

OR

BE A UNICORN YOURSELF?

WOULD YOU RATHER...

HAVE A MAGICAL FLYING CARPET

OR

A CAR THAT CAN FLY?

HAVE A FOOD FIGHT AGAINST YOUR PARENTS

OR

YOUR GRANDPARENTS?

WOULD YOU RATHER...

WAKE UP WITH KITTEN PAWS

OR

A GIANT MOUSE TAIL?

BE ABLE TO READ THE MINDS OF ANIMALS

OR

HUMANS?

WOULD YOU RATHER...

SPEND THE NIGHT IN AN ABANDONED AMUSEMENT PARK

OR

A HAUNTED HOUSE?

EAT PANCAKES FOR EVERY MEAL FOR A WEEK

OR

SPAGHETTI FOR EVERY MEAL FOR A MONTH?

WOULD YOU RATHER...

EVERY SINGLE THING YOU ATE FROM NOW ON TASTED LIKE POPCORN

OR

PIZZA?

HAVE A PET DRAGON THAT YOU HAVE TRAINED

OR

BE SOMEONE ELSE'S PET DRAGON THAT THEY TRAINED?

WOULD YOU RATHER...

HAVE WRIGGLING WORMS
FOR HAIR

OR

LARGE SNAILS FOR EARS?

HAVE THE POWER OF
INVISIBILITY

OR

BE ABLE TO LIVE FOREVER
AND NEVER GET OLD?

WOULD YOU RATHER...

NOT BE ABLE TO HEAR

OR

NOT BE ABLE TO SEE?

BE HALF HUMAN, HALF MACHINE

OR

HALF HUMAN, HALF ANIMAL?

WOULD YOU RATHER...

HAVE HANDS INSTEAD OF FEET

OR

FEET INSTEAD OF HANDS?

HAVE A NEVER-ENDING SUPPLY OF CANDY

OR

A NEVER-ENDING SUPPLY OF POPCORN?

WOULD YOU RATHER...

WAKE UP WITH A BALD EAGLE ON THE END YOUR BED

OR

3 RABBITS IN YOUR BED?

BE A CHARACTER IN YOUR FAVORITE GAME

OR

A CHARACTER IN YOUR FAVORITE MOVIE?

WOULD YOU RATHER...

ONLY BE ABLE TO DRINK JUICE

OR

ONLY BE ABLE TO DRINK SODA?

BE A POLICE OFFICER WITH A SQUEAKY VOICE

OR

A POLICE OFFICER WITH THE APPEARANCE OF A 10 YEAR OLD?

WOULD YOU RATHER...

SAIL IN A BOAT

OR

RIDE IN A HANG GLIDER?

HAVE SQUIRRELS FOR HANDS

OR

HAMSTERS FOR FEET?

WOULD YOU RATHER...

HAVE SIX LEGS

OR

SIX ARMS?

BE AN AVERAGE PERSON IN THE PRESENT

OR

A KING OR QUEEN OF A LARGE COUNTRY 800 YEARS AGO?

WOULD YOU RATHER...

BE AN ASTRONAUT

OR

A DEEP SEA DIVER?

BE ABLE TO READ ANY PERSON'S MIND

OR

BE ABLE TO LOOK INTO THE FUTURE?

WOULD YOU RATHER...

HOLD A POISONOUS SNAKE

OR

KISS A JELLYFISH?

HAVE A SHOWER THAT KEEPS YOU CLEAN FOR 7 DAYS

OR

HAVE A BED THAT GIVES YOU A FULL NIGHT'S REST IN ONE HOUR?

WOULD YOU RATHER...

BE A CHARACTER IN
FROZEN

OR

A CHARACTER IN
STAR WARS?

TRAVEL THE WORLD FOR
A YEAR

OR

GO TO THE INTERNATIONAL
SPACE STATION FOR A MONTH?

WOULD YOU RATHER...

EAT A SPOONFUL OF SALT

OR

A SPOONFUL OF PEPPER?

INVITE YODA TO A DINNER PARTY AT YOUR HOUSE

OR

JESUS TO A DINNER PARTY AT YOUR HOUSE?

WOULD YOU RATHER...

NEVER BE ABLE TO EAT WARM FOOD

OR

NEVER BE ABLE TO EAT COLD FOOD?

HAVE A SLIPPERY SLIDE TO GET DOWNSTAIRS

OR

HAVE A TRAMPOLINE TO GET UPSTAIRS?

WOULD YOU RATHER...

RIDE ON A
MOTORCYCLE

OR

A QUAD BIKE?

LIVE IN A HOUSE SHAPED
LIKE A CIRCLE

OR

A HOUSE SHAPED LIKE
A TRIANGLE?

WOULD YOU RATHER...

GO TO YOUR FIRST DAY AT A NEW SCHOOL IN YOUR GRANDMA'S CLOTHES

OR

DRESSED LIKE A BABY IN DIAPERS?

BE AN ASTRONAUT

OR

A RACE CAR DRIVER?

WOULD YOU RATHER...

BE ALLERGIC TO
PANCAKES

OR

ALLERGIC TO PIZZA?

HAVE A GIANT, MAGIC BALL
PIT IN YOUR HOUSE

OR

A SLIDE THAT GOES FROM YOUR
ROOF TO THE GROUND?

WOULD YOU RATHER...

HAVE A BOWLING ALLEY IN YOUR HOUSE

OR

A FREE MOVIE THEATRE NEXT TO YOUR HOUSE?

HAVE ALL DOGS TRY TO ATTACK YOU WHEN THEY SEE YOU

OR

ALL BIRDS TRY TO ATTACK YOU WHEN THEY SEE YOU?

WOULD YOU RATHER...

INSTANTLY BECOME A GROWN UP

OR

STAY THE AGE YOU ARE NOW FOR ANOTHER TWO YEARS?

ONLY EAT MCDONALDS FOR A MONTH

OR

ONLY EAT BURGER KING FOR A MONTH?

WOULD YOU RATHER...

MEET YOUR FUTURE SELF

OR

MEET YOUR FUTURE KIDS?

HAVE A PET KANGAROO THAT CAN SPEAK ENGLISH

OR

A PET DOG THAT IS BIG ENOUGH TO RIDE?

WOULD YOU RATHER...

NEVER HAVE ANY HOMEWORK

OR

BE PAID $3 PER HOUR FOR DOING YOUR HOMEWORK?

BE A ROBOT THAT COULD LIVE FOREVER

OR

A HUMAN WHO LIVES FOR 70 YEARS?

WOULD YOU RATHER...

BE THE AUTHOR OF A
POPULAR BOOK

OR

A MUSICIAN IN A
FAMOUS BAND?

HAVE YOUR ROOM REDECORATED
HOWEVER YOU WANT

OR

RECEIVE TEN VIDEO GAMES OF
YOUR CHOICE?

WOULD YOU RATHER...?

DANCE IN FRONT OF 1,000 PEOPLE

OR

SING IN FRONT OF 1,000 PEOPLE?

BE LOCKED IN A ROOM THAT IS CONSTANTLY DARK FOR A WEEK

OR

A ROOM THAT IS CONSTANTLY BRIGHT FOR A WEEK?

WOULD YOU RATHER...

HAVE AN AIR HOCKEY TABLE

OR

A PINBALL MACHINE?

ALWAYS BE REALLY EARLY EVERYWHERE YOU GO

OR

ALWAYS BE 20 MINUTES LATE?

WOULD YOU RATHER...

GO SNORKELING ON A REEF

OR

CAMPING BY A LAKE?

TRAIN A DINOSAUR SIZED CHICKEN

OR

TRAIN A CHICKEN SIZED DINOSAUR?

WOULD YOU RATHER...

ONLY BE ABLE TO JUMP
EVERYWHERE YOU GO

OR

ONLY BE ABLE TO WALK
ON YOUR HANDS?

WEAR FISH SMELLING CLOTHES
ON A FIRST DATE

OR

CLOTHES FIVE SIZES TOO BIG
ON LIVE TV?

WOULD YOU RATHER...

BE 4 FEET TALL

OR

8 FEET TALL?

GO SWIMMING IN A RIVER OF PINEAPPLE JUICE

OR

DIVE INTO A POOL OF MELTED ICE CREAM?

WOULD YOU RATHER...

RIDE IN A SMALL PLANE

OR

A LIMOUSINE?

COMMUNICATE ONLY USING SIGN LANGUAGE

OR

YELL REALLY LOUDLY WHENEVER YOU TALKED?

WOULD YOU RATHER...

LIVE AT AN AMUSEMENT PARK

OR

A BOWLING ALLEY?

ALWAYS TALK IN RHYMES

OR

ALWAYS SING INSTEAD OF SPEAKING?

WOULD YOU RATHER...

BRUSH YOUR TEETH
WITH SOAP

OR

DRINK SOUR MILK?

BE ALONE FOR THE REST OF
YOUR LIFE

OR

ALWAYS BE SURROUNDED BY
ANNOYING PEOPLE?

WOULD YOU RATHER...

HAVE A PERSONAL
LIFE-SIZED ROBOT

OR

A JETPACK?

BE ABLE TO CONTROL ALL
BIRDS WITH YOUR MIND

OR

ALL DOGS WITH YOUR MIND?

WOULD YOU RATHER...

LIVE IN AUSTRALIA

OR

LIVE IN AFRICA?

HAVE TO SKIP INSTEAD
OF WALK

OR

RUN REALLY FAST EVERYWHERE
YOU GO?

WOULD YOU RATHER...

BE AN AMAZING DANCER

OR

AN AMAZING SINGER?

LIVE ON A VERY HIGH MOUNTAIN

OR

ON A TROPICAL ISLAND?

WOULD YOU RATHER...

RIDE A GIANT ANT

OR

A GIGANTIC SNAKE?

SWIM 3 TIMES FASTER THAN
YOU CURRENTLY DO

OR

RUN 2 TIMES FASTER?

WOULD YOU RATHER...

VISIT THE MOON

OR

VISIT MARS?

TELL THE TRUTH AND
NOBODY BELIEVED YOU

OR

TELL LIES AND EVERYONE
BELIEVED YOU?

WOULD YOU RATHER...

LIVE IN THE MINECRAFT WORLD

OR

THE STAR WARS WORLD?

RIDE A BULL AT THE RODEO FOR 30 SECONDS

OR

SWIM WITH A SHARK FOR 10 SECONDS?

WOULD YOU RATHER...

DO SCHOOL WORK IN
A GROUP

OR

BY YOURSELF?

EAT SNAIL FLAVORED
ICE CREAM

OR

DRINK ROTTEN WORM
FLAVORED SODA?

WOULD YOU RATHER...

LOSE THE ABILITY TO READ

OR

LOSE THE ABILITY TO SPEAK?

BURP REALLY LOUDLY EVERY 5 MINUTES

OR

SNEEZE REALLY LOUDLY EVERY 5 MINUTES?

WOULD YOU RATHER...

BE ABLE TO TALK
TO DOGS

OR

CATS?

BRUSH YOUR TEETH WITH
YOUR FINGERS

OR

LET SOMEONE ELSE BRUSH
YOUR TEETH WITH THEIR
FINGERS?

HAVE ONE REALLY LONG LEG

OR

ONE REALLY LONG ARM?

A WEEK ON HOLIDAY WITH IRON MAN BUT YOU CAN'T TELL ANYONE

OR

2 DAYS WITH WONDER WOMAN AND YOU'RE ALLOWED TO TELL EVERYONE?

WOULD YOU RATHER...

BE THE ONLY CHILD

OR

HAVE 5 BROTHERS AND SISTERS?

EAT A ROTTEN FISH AND JELLY SANDWICH

OR

EAT A COCKROACH AND CHOCOLATE SANDWICH?

WOULD YOU RATHER...

DO YOUR OWN STUNTS IN AN ACTION MOVIE

OR

HAVE A STUNT PERSON DO THEM FOR YOU?

DRINK A CUP OF SEA WATER

OR

A CUP OF CLEAN WATER OUT OF YOUR TOILET?

WOULD YOU RATHER...

WASH YOUR HAIR WITH ORANGE JUICE

OR

BRUSH YOUR TEETH WITH KETCHUP?

HAVE A TINY DRAGON AS A SERVANT

OR

A LARGE DRAGON YOU CAN RIDE ON BUT IT HAS AN ANNOYING PERSONALITY?

WOULD YOU RATHER...

HAVE TWO COOKIES
EVERY DAY

OR

UNLIMITED COOKIES ONCE
A WEEK?

ONLY WEAR ONE COLOR
EACH DAY

OR

HAVE TO WEAR SEVEN
COLORS EACH DAY?

WOULD YOU RATHER...

RIDE IN A GIANT
KANGAROO'S POUCH

OR

ON THE BACK OF A GIANT
EAGLE?

MAKE A HOUSE OUT
OF BACON

OR

A FORT OUT OF
CHOCOLATE?

WOULD YOU RATHER...

BE ABLE TO CONTROL FIRE

OR

WATER?

LIVE ON THE BEACH

OR

IN A CABIN IN THE WOODS?

WOULD YOU RATHER...

EAT A LIVE
COCKROACH

OR

DRINK A GLASS OF
TOILET WATER?

BE BULLETPROOF

OR

BE ABLE TO SURVIVE FALLS
FROM ANY HEIGHT?

WOULD YOU RATHER...

VACATION IN FRANCE

OR

VACATION IN CANADA?

TAKE A CODING CLASS

OR

AN ART CLASS?

WOULD YOU RATHER...

WIN $100,000

OR

HAVE YOUR BEST FRIEND
WIN $1,000,000?

GET $5 EVERY TIME YOU
EAT A BRUSSEL SPROUT

OR

HAVE TO PAY $2 EVERY TIME
YOU EAT CHOCOLATE?

WOULD YOU RATHER...

CUDDLE AN ANGRY CHICKEN

OR

A RELAXED ALLIGATOR?

DRINK ALL YOUR FOOD
FROM A BABY BOTTLE

OR

WEAR VISIBLE DIAPERS FOR
THE REST OF YOUR LIFE?

WOULD YOU RATHER?

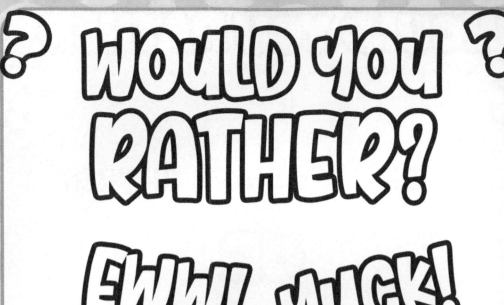

EWW! YUCK! GROSS!

This way to crazy, ridiculous and downright hilarious 'Would You Rathers?!'

WARNING!

These are Eww! These are Yuck! These are Gross! And they are really funny! Laughter awaits!

RatherFunnyPress.com

WOULD YOU RATHER...

PICK YOUR TEACHER'S NOSE

OR

CLIP THEIR TOENAILS?

HAVE A HAPPY, ELDERLY
GENTLEMAN FART
ON YOUR HEAD

OR

WEAR A DIRTY DIAPER
AS A HAT?

WOULD YOU RATHER...

EAT A SMALL CAN
OF CAT FOOD

OR

4 ROTTEN APPLES?

SMELL YOUR BEST
FRIEND'S BREATH

OR

HAVE THEM SMELL
YOUR BREATH?

WOULD YOU RATHER...

PEE YOUR PANTS
WHEN YOU LAUGH

OR

PEE YOUR PANTS
WHEN YOU CRY?

FART NEXT TO
YOUR GRANDMA

OR

YOUR GRANDMA FART
NEXT TO YOU?

WOULD YOU RATHER...

DRINK A SOGGY,
SQUISHED UP SLUG

OR

EAT A CRUNCHY, BAKED
COCKROACH?

HAVE WORMS COME OUT OF
YOUR NOSE WHEN YOU SNEEZE

OR

BE POOPED ON BY A
FLOCK OF PELICANS?

WOULD YOU RATHER...

EAT A BOWL OF
DEAD INSECTS

OR

A PIECE OF RAW MEAT?

STEP ON A POOP WHILE
RUNNING BAREFOOT
AT THE BEACH

OR

HAVE A POOP FLOAT BY
WHILE RELAXING IN
THE HOT TUB?

WOULD YOU RATHER...

SNIFF A CAT'S BUTT

OR

SNIFF A DOG'S BUTT?

HAVE A JOB POPPING
STRANGERS' PIMPLES

OR

PICKING THEIR NOSE AND
LICKING THEIR BOOGERS?

WOULD YOU RATHER...

GO DIVING WITH A SCUBA
TANK FULL OF FARTS

OR

WEE ON AN
ELECTRIC FENCE?

LICK THE CLASSROOM
FLOOR

OR

LICK THE BOTTOM OF YOUR
TEACHER'S SHOE?

WOULD YOU RATHER...

LICK YOUR BEST
FRIEND'S EYEBALL

OR

EAT A ROTTEN TOMATO?

SIT IN A HOT TUB FULL OF
SNAILS AND WORMS

OR

SWIM IN A POOL FULL OF
ROTTEN FISH?

WOULD YOU RATHER...

WATCH A MOVIE ABOUT THE HISTORY OF FARTS

OR

THE HISTORY OF POO?

EAT A BIG MAC YOU FOUND IN A GARBAGE BIN

OR

A CHOCOLATE BAR YOU FOUND IN A MUDDY PUDDLE?

WOULD YOU RATHER...

EAT A TEASPOON OF
OLD LADY BOOGERS

OR

A SMALL BOWL OF
DEAD FLIES?

CONTROL THE SMELL OF
YOUR FART SO IT
SMELLS LIKE APPLE PIE

OR

THE SOUND OF YOUR FART
SO IT SOUNDS LIKE
A LION ROARING?

THANKS A BUNCH!

For reading our book!
We hope you have enjoyed these
'WOULD YOU RATHER?'
scenarios as much as we did as we were
putting this book together.
If you could possibly leave a review of our
book we would really appreciate it. 😊
To see all our latest books or leave a review
just go to
RatherFunnyPress.com
Once again, thanks so much for reading!

P.S. If you enjoyed the bonus chapter,
EWW! YUCK! GROSS!
you can always check out our brand new book,

WOULD YOU RATHER?
EWW! YUCK! GROSS!
for hundreds of brand new, crazy and ridiculous
scenarios that are sure to get the kids rolling on the
floor with laughter!
Just go to:
RatherFunnyPress.com
Thanks again! 😊

YOUR
FREE SURPRISE GIFT!

To grab your free copy of this brand new, hilarious Joke Book, just go to:

go.RatherFunnyPress.com

Enjoy!

RatherFunnyPress.com

Printed in Great Britain
by Amazon